A-Z of better brand language

Rob Self-Pierson

Foreword by John Simmons

THE BRAND LANGUAGE STUDIO

A-Z of better brand language

Rob Self-Pierson
The Brand Language Studio

www.thebrandlanguage.studio

Copyright © 2021 Rob Self-Pierson
Design and illustrations by Karina Stolf

Printed and bound in Great Britain by Ingram Spark

ISBN 978-0-9933234-2-3

A CIP catalogue record for this book is available from the British Library.

"Where people aren't having any fun,
they seldom produce good work."

David Ogilvy

Foreword

"Pick a card. Any card." Opening this book is a bit like being invited to take part in a magic trick. But instead of a card, pick a letter, any letter.

I went randomly to the letter F, where I read that F is for Feeling, and in a few short sentences I was drawn into a story of a man who had lost his father. As Rob suggests, language is emotion; I've always thought that too. Words connect us to our feelings – and one writer's words can make that connection happen.

Only connect, I often say. Successful brands understand the power of that relationship between words and emotions, and writers for brands need to know how to use that power. Good writers can be unashamedly emotional because they know that this makes the connection to people. Which is what every brand wants: connection that builds trust, engagement and loyalty.

Cold, hard facts are useful but they will only take you so far. F is for Feeling, writes Rob. He could have written F is for Facts, but he made a choice that expresses his belief. Writers always have a choice when they are using words, and this book will encourage you to be truthful as well as playful when making such choices.

Words can do so much. In We, Me, Them & It I put it like this: "Words can move, explain, startle, excite, persuade, express ideas... and more."

Rob understands this. He understands it intuitively and also from years of experience honing his skills in writing for brands. He knows that one word leads to another, and that often it's the surprise that counts (for writer and reader); that words are containers of meaning and feeling; that they have to be nurtured with love and pride and respect. Words are your children: look after them well.

Rob looks after his words in this elegant book. Given the chance, he will look after yours too. Read this book from A through to Z, or dip into it at random, and you will be charmed and stimulated.

So go on, pick a card. You've already got the ace of diamonds.

John Simmons
Author, language mentor & poet
2021

Introduction

More than any other ingredient, language has the power to transform an organisation.

The right words can start a business on a path to profitability, encourage teams to work smarter and more productively, and inspire consumers to shout about a brand to their friends.

Handled with deep care and respect, as you might a family heirloom or shiny new smart phone, a brand's language can help an organisation to speak with great clarity, character and consistency – whether it's a tiny charity or an enormous multinational.

For many years, my studio has supported brands around the world with language. We've named products, articulated purpose, and worded value propositions. We've developed tones of voice, told founders' stories, produced websites and scripts and brochures and straplines and more. You name it, we've written it. From Gumtree to Moorlands College, we've seen countless times how words change brands. But we've also seen how learning to embrace language can change a person's life.

We were reminded this recently by somebody we trained at Gumtree in 2015. The young woman, a business graduate at the time, emailed to say a piece of advice we'd shared in a tone of voice workshop – simply to remember that there is no B2B and B2C, only human to human – had gone on to influence a presentation she'd made to a business partner. The presentation had gone well. So well in fact she'd been offered the chance to join the other company. She told us, in language alive with delight, that she would soon be starting a new job and new life with her family on a continent far away.

Words matter. They can help us to connect with people, to grow relationships with them, and to reveal or create new opportunities, in business and in life. But how?

Curious to know what makes language effective – especially in the world of business and brand – we looked back at and analysed our most successful projects. We also reconnected with some of the many hundreds of people we've trained over the years. Staff at all levels of organisations we've sat with, taught writing techniques to, and supported to become more confident, happy and skilled writers. If they could pass on their own advice from a new-found love of working with words, what would that advice be?

The A-Z in your hands reveals the findings: things we noticed, and things we heard. It shines a light on those tools, beliefs and attitudes that affect how an organisation and its people use language, behave as a result, and are later perceived, both inside and outside the office.

Much of what we found surprised us. Instead of lots of tips on better craft, a great deal of the advice you'll find here is about approach. Trade secrets on how to prepare for a language project, to win over doubters, to inspire colleagues, and to manage things towards success. Of course there's also advice on how to improve your writing practice. What use an A-Z of better brand language without that?

This book's for you if you work in a creative agency and write, or manage someone who does. Perhaps you're a junior copywriter low on confidence, a graphic designer feeling out of their depth when asked to come up with copy, or a creative director looking to spark their team with new ideas. Equally, if you're a small business owner curious to know how language can help your brand, or a chief exec at a global firm determined to improve your company's most crucial messaging, we're confident there's plenty to inspire you too.

For each letter of the alphabet, we've also created a brand language exercise so you can put what you learn into practice straightaway. There's no right or wrong response – just give them a go. We hope each stretches and rewards you.

Right, it's time to join us in the wonderful world of brand language. Are you ready?

A is for

Why write at all if not to move another person to think, to feel, to act, or most often in the commercial world to buy or believe?

You'd be amazed by how often the words you speak and write change the way other people live their lives. To move a consumer or client or perhaps an investor to buy or believe, your writing will need to connect with them. At an emotional level. To do that, you first need to get close to their experience. Who are they? What do they do? How are they feeling today? The more you know, or work hard to imagine, the easier you'll find it to write for your audience – not just for yourself, which is easily done.

Think of it like this. You're keen to show a friend, relative or loved one you care for them. That they're the most important person in your life. Do you cook their favourite dish or your own?

Give it a go
Do a pencil sketch of your reader. Give them a name, age, some life experiences. Note their loves, hates, passions and pains. What they're doing today, how they're feeling. Now write for them. How does getting to know your audience affect your words?

Audience

B is for

Language has the power to transform an organisation. We believe that from our writing fingers to our toes. You need to believe it too.

Studies show that language affects how people make decisions. Behavioural science has even put numbers to it. But mostly you'll be taking and encouraging others to take author Rory Sutherland's 'creative leap of faith'. You'll be asking business people – with their right/wrong and profit/loss – to invest in something creative, with its, "Maybe we could try..." When you do, you need to believe so wholeheartedly in what you say that your enthusiasm persuades others.

Keep in mind the words of the late HRH Prince Philip, here talking about The Duke of Edinburgh's Award: "When you start something, you don't really know if it's going to work or not." Often, all you have is your strength of belief.

Give it a go
When things are going well, write a positive message to yourself. Something to encourage you at tougher times, and to remind you of all the wonderful possibilities of language. Which words do you use to capture what you believe so deeply?

Belief

C is for

Writing is as creative as art and design. That's especially important to remember in business, where constraints mean you need to think lateral and fast.

But brand language too often lacks creativity. Words slouch on the page or screen, shoulders slumped and faces long. They appear as the forgotten relation of novels, poems, scripts and other 'creative writing'. But the words you write for brands crave the colour you give a tweet, the energy you give a text. They need original thought, inspired imagination and bold decisions. Treating your writing as a creative art, while keeping focused on your audience, will help you write the sort of copy people never forget.

We wonder why only designers are the 'creatives'. Perhaps writers are the magicians. With the swish of a pen, you have the chance to influence the way people think, feel, act, speak and live their lives.

Give it a go
In response to a brief, write the blurb of a book. In one short paragraph, share the best bits of the brand, bank card, uni course etc. Be playful, colourful, conjure language to tease your reader. How has a creative exercise influenced your approach?

Creativity

D is for

Decisiveness isn't about getting things right. It's about being bold enough to make decisions because you think, feel or sense it's for the best.

Brand language can suffer from what one of our clients calls the 'washing machine effect'. A piece of writing goes around and around, from draft to draft, department to department, until it loses all its shape, colour and personality. Nobody, not even the creator of the brief, is bold enough to sign it off. We understand why it happens – because writing's tough, and knowing what's 'right' isn't much easier. But an endless spin will harm the project.

Brand language requires strong decisions. Like in a brand story, which character to focus on. In a brand purpose, the key reason to exist. In a sentence, which word to begin with. Always remember: one strong decision will inspire the next.

Give it a go
In your next meeting, when you sense the washing machine door closing, be the person to make the decision. Be honest: say it feels right, you can't be sure, but "let's try it and make it work". How does being decisive affect the people around you?

Decisiveness

E is for

Those who write should be curious, no, ravenous for new experiences. The more life you live, the richer your writing and happier your reader.

Travel is ideal with its new sights, smells, sounds, tastes, textures, colours; how one moment it fills you with excitement, the next with uncertainty. Travel can be a flight around the world or a short walk to a new café. Exploring art, reading poetry, taking part in courses. Meeting friends, strolling in nature, paying attention to your senses. These are all ways to live and gain experience to enhance your writing. Anything, in the words of Robert Frost, to "trip [you] head foremost into the boundless".

A friend set up Culture Shock at her agency. Once a month, somebody in the team would book tickets to an event. The purpose was always to enjoy a new and thought-provoking experience.

Give it a go

Buy tickets to something you know little about. Go with your notepad and pen. Be there, immersed in the experience but aware. On your way home, write five lines beginning, "Tonight I..." What thoughts and language has the new experience provoked?

Experiences

F is for

Language is emotion. Through words, or in their absence, we communicate what we feel deep in our hearts. This is also true for brands.

At least brands have the opportunity. But what copy has moved you recently? What piece of advertising or packaging has made you stop, think and feel? Brands are our companions in our highest highs and most tragic lows. Their words have the potential to celebrate with us or put their arms around our shoulders. It's up to those behind brands, people like you and me, to push beyond corporate blah until we connect with people in a deep, meaningful way.

We once helped to reposition a design studio. In a conversation around purpose, the founder shared the story of losing his father. Through tears, the real reason for living a creative life emerged. We used this emotion to suggest a purpose and position.

Give it a go
Write about a defining moment in your life, perhaps about somebody you've loved or lost. Just this once, forget audience – this one's for you. Focus on your feelings; if you can, write through strong emotions. How is this writing different to your brand work?

Feeling

G is for

For every child inspired by English lessons at school, there are ten times more left terrified by all the rules. Fact: schoolbook English ain't everything.

Grammar here stands for punctuation, spelling, tenses and so on. Those technical aspects of writing that come later, when you're so obsessed with craft you find yourself reading style guides by moonlight. They're crucial to master for every copywriter who's publishing work. But you strategists and creative directors, designers and project managers, and people of all ages at all levels of every organisation, don't let bad school memories stop you writing.

I developed writing workshops for primary school kids learning from home. Teaching a dyslexic girl taught me how scary writing can seem. Working to Milly's strengths – such joy, enthusiasm and imagination! – we made writing playful and safe.

Give it a go
Write down the language rules you remember from school. Like, "Don't start a sentence with 'And'." In response to a brief, but in the safety of a notepad, break every one. Enjoy the freedom, but be aware of the rules you break. Which help and which harm?

Grammar

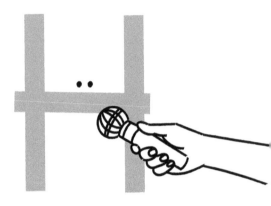

H is for

'Authenticity' is today's buzzword in brand and business. Every agency seems to encourage every client to be authentic. Perhaps 'honesty' is better.

An honest brand writes in a tone that truly reflects its personality, on subjects it feels truly passionate about, using words it believes will truly connect. Like an honest person, the brand shares good and bad in equal measure. But – and here's the crucial bit – sharing honestly takes great craft. Because honest opinions aren't always the easiest for others to hear. Honest language is 20% preparation, 20% writing and 60% editing. When your heart pumps faster and skin begins to tingle, it's time to publish.

Not to say being authentic is bad. But focusing only there can lead to an obsession with self, an 'us-first' approach. Where being honest will encourage you to consider how your words affect others.

Give it a go
Write your own 'brand' proposition. Be totally honest about who you are, what you do and why you do it. It could be about you in business or in life. Edit, edit, edit to make sure you mean every word you write. What does a focus on honesty do to your writing?

Honesty

I is for

Inspiration exists all around us. It is abundant, in what we read, hear, see, smell, taste, reach out for, shy away from and stumble upon.

To make a great success of your language project, look for inspiration in all things, always, including: conversation; novels; poetry; forests; beaches; art; wildlife; documentaries; exercise; music; museums; films; fear; science; silence; people; travel; clouds; space; even what you had for breakfast today. In the reflection of a raindrop, there is enough to inspire the greatest campaign you'll ever write. Just remember: inspiration is kindest to those who are wide-eyed and welcoming to the world around them.

Some clients ask us only to analyse competition for inspiration. "See their success? Let's do it like them." In brand language, competitor analysis is crucial for many reasons. Inspiration is rarely one.

Give it a go
Stumped by a brief? Go for a walk with eyes wide and mind open. Perhaps ask a stranger a question. Think freely. Allow thoughts to become ideas. Later, visit a bookshop or library or go online to research any new themes. What has your walk inspired?

Inspiration

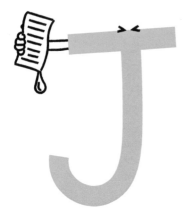

J is for

To make a brand absolutely irresistible through language, you need to learn how to squeeze every sentence you write for juice. But how?

Make sure that each word contributes to meaning, feeling or rhythm. Choose verbs and adjectives with care; be sure they communicate what you mean. Avoid adverbs, unless they enhance your writing dramatically. Vary sentence length for pace and punch. Use repetition for effect. Sow metaphors that later bloom. And, when you're sure it's right for your subject and reader, use that most powerful of story-telling techniques. The one great authors and script-writers use to thrill an audience. To get them to turn pages and tune in next week. Withholding.

Master these advanced techniques and you'll find new ways to refresh your reader when you write. Watch and smile as they come back for more.

Give it a go
Find and print something you've written that never thrilled you. Use the tips above to highlight what's juicy and what's not. Now edit your writing until you're confident every word will refresh your reader. How do your before and after compare?

Juice

K is for

To write you need to know. Or at least put in lots of effort to get to know – go places, investigate subjects, interview from the bottom of an organisation up.

"First thing we would do is get so damn absorbed into that business we would almost own it." That's how Jim Durfee, copywriter at Carl Ally Inc, puts it in Doug Pray's excellent documentary Art & Copy. Jim talks about his team's energy, curiosity and fascination that led to the launch and rapid growth of brands like FedEx. The trick to writing about a subject you don't know well – which is a situation writers find themselves in pretty much every project – is to immerse yourself almost entirely.

But not entirely. Because then you'll suffer like the brand you're there to help. You should be so close you can smell the skin, but detached enough to be able to describe it in powerful and original language.

Give it a go
Ask someone to give you a subject they love but you know nothing about, like their favourite band. Spend 55 minutes researching, making notes, then five minutes writing in any form. What did extreme immersion and a writing blast help you to create?

Knowledge

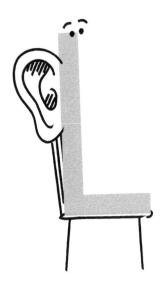

L is for

We've stolen all our best brand language. Wait. No. Not quite stolen. But transcribed, almost verbatim, from chats with our clients and their consumers.

Take BSV, a company in Australia that installs big screen technology. We ran a workshop to help position the brand and differentiate it through its language. In conversation, almost whispered, the marketing exec said to us, "We're in the business of bringing spaces to life." Six weeks later, 'Bringing spaces to life' was BSV's strapline, proposition opener and lead web copy. We used it to develop not only brand positioning, but values and tone of voice. How did we come up with it? We listened.

There's lots online about active listening, where you pay full attention to someone, and passive listening, where you don't. To us, that's the difference between listening and hearing. Be a writer who listens.

Give it a go
Next time you're in a café, listen for phrases that float between the clinking cups. Focus your ears on words around you, like you focus your eyes on the page or screen when you read. Which sentences speak to you, and why?

Listening

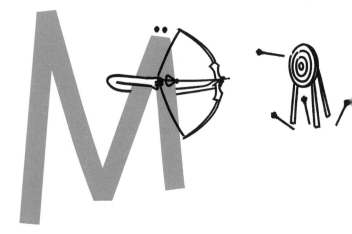

M is for

Working with language isn't easy. You're going to make mistakes. Accept that as a fact, keep going when it's tough, and pay attention to improve.

You might get grammar, punctuation or spelling wrong. You might make a decision that doesn't pay off – thinking the brief requires this, when really it wants that. In key presentations, you might mix metaphors, contradict yourself, spot a typo or fluff the killer line you rehearsed many times. It happens. To every writer. When it does, you can feel ashamed and give up. Or you can realise no brand language project has ever been ruined by such mistakes.

The biggest mistake you can make – the one that's guaranteed to jeopardise success – is to doubt the power of language. Please don't do it. Remember: you're a magician. Your words can influence how people think, feel, act, speak and live their lives.

Give it a go
Write an email to yourself about a mistake you once made, in language or life. Give details about what happened, share how you felt, and explain what you learned. Press send. How does receiving this positive reframing of a mistake make you feel?

Mistakes

N is for

Airbnb's 'Belong Anywhere' slogan helps people feel like a local wherever they travel. To improve as a writer, we feel it's better to belong nowhere.

That way you remain an outsider, looking into the brand world of others with innocent eyes. You see things they don't, in language uncharted. Immerse yourself in subjects, of course, but come up for air. If a client invites you to drinks to help you feel you belong, be there but aware. Remember you are a nomad, excited to visit but reluctant to become too at home. Design consultant Michael Wolff once told us: "Experience leads to comfort, my biggest enemy. It fools me into thinking I know what I'm doing."

You can encourage clients to embrace the nomadic approach. We prefer to run workshops in a venue far from their comfort zone. They're often amazed at the language they discover away from home.

Give it a go
Next creative meeting with your team or client, pick an unexpected venue. A local record shop for a global bank, street market for a tech start-up. Each exercise, encourage people to be outside looking in. How does it influence the words they choose?

Nomadic

O is for

Search engines are terrific for finding answers to questions. But the straight line from curiosity to knowledge can also be terribly limiting.

A colleague said Google was her go-to for inspiration. She'd search for the subject and work from results. One day we asked her to close the computer, leave her phone on her desk, take a notepad and pen, and walk. She should explore the streets around our studio until something intrigued or excited her. It would be her subject. Reflecting on what she found, and what she imagined, she should write. If ever she craved Google, she should try to understand why.

Our writer returned with original scribbles – the sort of goodness that exists between an online search and its results. It was rich in imagery and metaphor, a fresh take on a subject with a million hits. Our writer said she now understood the power of offline.

Give it a go
Next brief, start research offline. It might mean going to a site, phoning people, buying a book. It's likely to be a slower, more involved process. That's good. Only use the internet to enhance your research, not start it. How has going offline changed your writing?

Offline

P is for

When you play in language, you make unique and powerful discoveries. The more freely you play, the more valuable the things you find.

We talk about the Inner Critic in writing – that voice in your head that tells you what you create is stupid, bad or wrong. Play in language and there is no stupid, bad or wrong. How could there be? It would be like telling a child in a sandpit they're not doing it right. Play with rhythm and rhyme, with pace and structure. Play with word order and sentence lengths. Play among the letters until you write something that makes you smile. Witness how your Inner Critic gets quieter the more fun you have.

"If you're not in a state of play, you can't make anything." That's the view of Paula Scher, one of the world's most influential graphic designers, speaking on Netflix's brilliant series Abstract.

Give it a go
Write a letter to your Inner Critic sharing your views on the importance of play. Show how having fun with words helps a writer to discover new ways to connect. Remember the Critic is full of doubt. How can your words help them to think differently?

Play

Q is for

To uncover the nuance and detail that makes brand language compelling, you need to be as curious as a journalist on the brink of their biggest story.

Say you're writing about a new-style guitar. Don't just say what it looks like. Interview the inventor to discover the origins of its every ingredient, from the spider-web strings to pumpkin polish. Where did her passion for guitars start? What inspired her design of this amp-shattering model? Did anything almost force her to give up? Why did she perservere? Her answers will reveal lots about the product and brand. When wrapping up your interview and everyone's relaxed, ask a final question. Make it your deepest.

In a room of experts, be the person to ask the stupid question. In doing so you'll break the tension, realise there's no such thing as a stupid question, and find that half the experts know less than you.

Give it a go
Become the ghost writer of your favourite celebrity's autobiography. Do your research, then spend time writing the questions you're going to ask them. Start on the surface and get deeper. Remember, emotion makes connections. How deep can you go?

Question

R is for

The best writing advice I know was offered to me by communications consultant Tim Rich: "To be kind to your reader, be ruthless in your edits."

Masters of brand language tend to be ruthless editors. Reading their own or others' work, they spot where to cut unnecessary words. They remove or reinvent clichés. They refine metaphors, making sure each is original and arresting. To check their edits are improving their writing, they read it out loud. Does it flow? Could it be simpler to say, more satisfying to follow? Like a sculptor, the best writers continue until their work is smooth and elegant.

Read your own writing out loud. If you stumble, even just a little, chip and gouge and rasp and polish until your words flow. If you're getting ready to publish, don't be satisfied with 'It's probably ok'. Remember: to be kind to your reader, be ruthless in your edits.

Give it a go
Get a first draft down quickly. Fine if you feel it's a jagged block of stone. Now step away, ideally for a day though a few hours is ok. Return to edit ruthlessly, aiming to reduce the word count by 20%. How has a focused edit improved your writing?

Ruthlessness

S is for

Great writing, whether a Murakami short story or classic 1960s VW ad from Bill Bernbach and his team, offers its reader many moments of surprise.

Corporate reports can too. Even your Ts and Cs. In everything you ever write, at work and at home, you have the opportunity to move your reader with a little unexpected. It might be a striking image that splashes colour over a grey subject. A dance of rhythm – some alliteration? Perhaps a rhyming pair? – that changes the pace following a passage of pathos. It could be telling a brand story so deeply honest that your reader is made speechless, seeing themselves in the descriptions you write.

On top of moving your audience, surprises will help you to first win their attention. They might even secure your next contract. Because it's often these moments that leave the most memorable mark.

Give it a go
Find VW's 'Lemon' ad from 1960. Highlight the different ways its copywriter has surprised you. Try to work out how they've done it. Now write a similar ad for a brand or product you love. How can you surprise your reader to keep them engaged?

Surprises

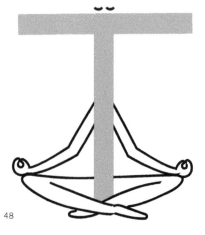

T is for

Writing with a pen in your hand and notepad on your knee can seem slow. Clunky perhaps. Old-fashioned even. From our experience, it's the better way.

And recent studies support us. According to the Wall Street Journal, handwriting "can improve idea composition and expression". Writing for Headspace, the mindfulness app, neuroscientist Dr Claudia Aguirre celebrates how handwriting helps you to focus on what's important – after all, it's tricky to get distracted when you're busy crafting letterforms. Dr Claudia goes on to describe a recently discovered neural pathway only activated when we draw letters. It's linked to better learning and memory.

So, handwriting. With its touch and feel. It can spark your best ideas, help you to focus on what's important, and improve how you learn and remember. Three essentials for any brand writer.

Give it a go
Look around your room for a smallish object. Pick it up, hold it, feel it. Look closely at its details. Now write about it – pen on paper – in any short form. Focus on what you feel is important to communicate. How does touch influence the way you write?

U is for

Perhaps you have an image of a writer in your head. She's sitting at her desk in the corner of a room lit by lamplight. She's still, focused, lost in thought.

She exists! We know plenty of writers who work this way, happiest in their own company. But many brand writers we love to work with are at their most creative and productive when around others. They get energy from meeting consumers, sparring with designers, discussing scenarios with strategists, or working directly with a client. They might head to a café or back to their desk to craft the writing. But their ideas come from being part of a team.

On top of boosting creative ideas, working together can keep energy levels up. We all lose belief. It's easier (and more fun) to carry on when you're supported by keen, creative folk who believe in you and the importance of what you're doing.

Give it a go
Write a profile of somebody you love collaborating with. Perhaps they're a designer or a musician. Celebrate what you admire about them, and how your work benefits from theirs. How can a sense of unity, of creating as a team, improve your writing?

Unity

V is for

Add craft to your writing to improve your brand's language. Develop a distinctive tone of voice and you'll transform the fortunes of your organisation.

Wise brands know this. Gumtree, who years earlier had invented the online classifieds category, was losing market share to playful start-ups. With uni fees rocketing, the British Council's matter-of-fact messaging was failing to attract international students to the UK. As Covid devastated families and forced children into orphanages, Hope and Homes's polite messages were being lost among thousands of charities desperate to fund change. At a time of make or break, each brand turned to tone of voice.

A voice that's true to a brand, relevant and engaging can reinforce positioning, express character, bring clarity to messages, make new connections and boost culture, as staff feel inspired to write.

Give it a go
Imagine you're the creative director of your favourite brand. To get a sense of tone, note patterns in recent comms: word choice, sentence length, metaphors. It's time to brief your new writer. Which tonal qualities will help him be true, relevant and engaging?

Voice

W is for

Pursuing perfection drags too many language projects to an unsatisfying halt. Surely it's better to live happily in 'perfect imperfection'?

That's what life coach Beth Kempton writes about so eloquently in her book Wabi Sabi. Though impossible to translate directly, this Japanese concept is to see beauty in the rough, unfinished or ugly-to-many. Traditionally, wabi sabi is experienced in the ever-evolving wonders of nature. Great creative directors live by wabi sabi. In the messy scribbles and scamps of their writers and designers, they spot the brilliance of creative work that goes on to change the way we live. You can learn to write the wabi sabi way.

Go panning in old notes for nuggets of goodness. In drafts you hate, save phrases others love. When a route is rejected, don't just delete it. Walk along it again looking for language with another life.

Give it a go
Find a draft you threw out because someone told you it wasn't right or good enough, like a rejected name. Being both playful and ruthless, create a new brand that it's perfectly imperfect for. How can work you once looked down on inspire something special?

Wabi sabi

X is for

Sometimes there are no words. Sometimes as a writer – similar to being the frontperson of a band – you should learn to be silent and still.

It gives space for others, your 'brandmates', to find ways to connect. Say a brief lands asking for a script to guide a short film about loss. Wouldn't allowing the film team freedom to capture raw stories be more powerful? A travel agent wants a strapline to qualify a photograph of a paradise island. Surely the photographer's work speaks more clearly without? Often the most powerful language is in the story a mind shares with itself in the absence of words.

Learn from brands who know this. Study them. Take them to bed. "Become so obsessed you can't sleep," as John Jessup, advertising creative, once told us. The more aware you become of words, the quicker you'll realise when they're not needed.

Give it a go
Find a photo you feel tells a story. Put it away and write something in response to what you've seen. Now look at your writing beside the photograph. Could anything you've written enhance the image, or is it more powerful without words?

Y is for

Curiosity killed the cat. Not the writer. The more often you say 'yes' than 'no' in life, the more you, your writing and your reader will be rewarded.

Personally, saying 'yes' has led me to study in California, aged 19 and clueless. To travel Britain and Europe and publish the memoirs. To visit Nigeria for a spectacular wedding, to write poetry below Mount Fuji, to go freelance, start a studio, and now to write this A-Z. Every adventure has provided my writing with the deep richness of experience, energy and emotion. I sometimes wonder where I'd be today if I'd said 'no' instead. Ever wondered the same?

Be a 'YES!' writer. Agree to projects that scare you. Visit cities that make you nervous. Be curious, uncertain and vulnerable. Put your feelings into everything you write; hold nothing back. With each bold step, pay attention to how you grow as a writer.

Give it a go
Next time someone invites you to try something scary, say 'YES!' As you're doing the new thing, be aware of how it makes you feel. When you're ready, write about it. How does this curious, uncertain and vulnerable approach influence your writing?

Z is for

Too many brand language projects fizzle out. It can be a lack of belief, a fear of mistakes, not enough play, perhaps it's the washing machine effect...

It might just be that writing is difficult. As Ernest Hemingway most likely said: "There's nothing to writing. All you do is sit down at a typewriter and open a vein." A heartfelt note to staff or press release about a crucial business decision can take great emotional energy to write. A big presentation can seem so terrifying it zaps you. Sometimes – especially in the heat of a crisis – crafting the right message can feel so tough it reduces you to tears. At these times, you might question whether you're good enough to carry on.

The answer is yes, you are. There's strength within and around you. Use it to write through doubts and fears. Mark every success. Then write some more.

Give it a go
Raise a glass to that tone of voice launch. Tweet your joy at a winning pitch. Glow in the knowledge that through writing and sharing your words you've achieved something huge. What does marking even the smallest success do to your writing spirit?

Zeal

Only connect

Are you curious to find out more about how language can transform your organisation?

Read our articles on brand, language and brand language over at **thebrandlanguage.studio**. Email us on **hello@thebrandlanguage.studio** and start a conversation. Or see our latest updates on LinkedIn and Instagram **@thebrandlanguagestudio**.

We hope to meet you soon. But for now go, play, make magic and enjoy creating better brand language.

Writing even better

We reference brilliant people and their books in the A-Z. Here they are in alphabetical order, plus others we're confident you'll get lots from:

• • •

Alchemy
by Rory Sutherland

The Brand Gap
by Marty Neumeier

Damn Good Advice
by George Lois

How To Live (collection)
by Thich Nhat Hanh

The Unpublished David Ogilvy
by David Ogilvy

Wabi Sabi
by Beth Kempton

We, Me, Them & It
by John Simmons

Write To The Point
by Sam Leith

• • •

Also, check out the series **Abstract** on Netflix, and the documentary **Art & Copy** by Doug Pray.

Lightning Source UK Ltd.
Milton Keynes UK
UKHW021556111221
395443UK00006B/311